BLEEDING HEARTS
LOVE POEMS FOR THE NERVOUS AND HIGHLY STRUNG.

Editorial assistants: Kristina Blagojevitch
and Nikiforos Doxiadis Mardas, with special thanks to Nicola Carr
Contributing editor: Melissa Stein
Technical editor: Brian Burns
Designed by Michelle Lovric and AB3
Internal collages by Jenny Lovric
Flowers from The Wild Bunch, Covent Garden
Produced by Imago
Manufactured in China

10 9 8 7 6 5 4 3 2 1

First published by Aurum Press Ltd.

First U.S. Edition

ISBN 0-312-19168-5

Other recent titles by Michelle Lovric:

Deadlier Than the Male
(St Martin's Press, 1997)

The Miseries of Human Life
(St Martin's Press, 1996)

BLEEDING
HEARTS

We have hearts within,
Warm, live, improvident, indecent hearts.

Elizabeth Barrett Browning (1806–61)
English poet

BLEE
HEAR

DING
TS

Love Poems
for the Nervous
& Highly Strung
edited by Michelle Lovric

St. Martin's Press
New York

Foreword

I think we ought to read only the kind of books that wound and stab us . . . We need the books that affect us like a disaster, that grieve us deeply, like the death of someone we loved more than ourselves, like being banished into forests far from everyone, like a suicide. A book must be the axe for the frozen sea inside us.

Franz Kafka (1883–1924)
Czech writer
from a letter to Oskar Pollak, January 27th, 1904.

It is an unrespectable tradition that most anthologies about Love invest it with an unalloyed deliciousness that is supposedly sweeter than chocolate. For late twentieth-century practitioners, Love is much less a smooth swoon of luscious lyricism than a neurotic emergency. Love is an unrelenting appetite that engorges or debilitates the organs and the senses. The lover suffers equally from starvation and indigestion, and is equally frightened of both.

Bleeding Hearts addresses these issues with a selection of truly neurotic and tortured love poetry—poems for the mean times, for the broken hearts, for the trampled hopes and for the rare and fragile outbreaks of nervous optimism. This is the Woody Allen School of Love: tragic, funny, irreverent and surprisingly sexy.

This is a book for anyone who has binged on the saccharine songs of love, for anyone who has ever waited by the phone, for anyone too afraid to start again—anyone who plans somehow to survive the agony and angst of Modern Love.

Michelle Lovric, Covent Garden, January 1998.

Contents

Prologue

Complaints and confessions of a poem

I am a poem and I dislike poets.
I detest their sneaking way of approaching
the blank sacrificial paper with a plague
of hearty inquisitors, auditors and valuers
up their crowded sleeves.
The first thing you notice about them
is their well-stocked acquisitive eyes
that is what makes them so intense,
so pensive and so *introverted* as the saying goes.
Watch them squat over heart, furniture or nature
with shark-infested crystal balls
missing nothing, catching everything,
piling all that stuff on my back,
including those carnivorous
punctuation-signs that make me
itch all over like a scabious dog.
Nothing is neglected. The ordained inventory
goes on with a conveyor-belt's consistency—
row upon row of lovely lines, beautifully
chiselled doubts, clipped words of despair
beautifully susurrated by intricate lips.

I act the part of a printed dustbin,
a receptacle for petty deaths and puny resurrections,
festooned traumas and festering roses,
dung and super dung.

I am a poem, I know—
I am here for all to see:
a rotting absence
lying in state in dark aspic.

If you're a poem like me
and a poet rings your bell,
do not answer, play dead.

Feyyaz Fergar (1919–93) Turkish poet, writer and translator

Poetry is a way of taking life by the throat. Robert Frost (1874–1963)

NEVER OFFER YOUR HEART

TO SOMEONE WHO EATS HEARTS

Love and Fear

What the heart is like

Officially the heart
is oblong, muscular,
and filled with longing.

But anyone who has painted the heart knows
that it is also

spiked like a star
and sometimes bedraggled
like a stray dog at night
and sometimes powerful
like an archangel's drum.

And sometimes cube-shaped
like a draughtsman's dream
and sometimes gaily round
like a ball in a net.

And sometimes like a thin line
and sometimes like an explosion.

And in it is
only a river,
a weir
and at most one little fish
by no means golden.

More like a grey
jealous
loach.

It certainly isn't noticeable
at first sight.

Anyone who has painted the heart knows
that first he had to
discard his spectacles,
his mirror,
throw away his fine-point pencil
and carbon paper

and for a long while
walk
outside.

Miroslav Holub (b. 1923)
Czech poet and scientist
Translated by Ewald Osers

it is true
there is love that
is decided upon
and love that spreads like a stain
of ink in absorbent cloth
there is love
that makes sense of your life
and love that makes you senseless
about life

Diane Wakoski (b. 1937)
American poet

10

A Prayer from *A Common Prayer*

There are only two feelings. Love and fear.
There are only two languages. Love and fear.
There are only two activities. Love and fear.
There are only two motives, two procedures,
two frameworks, two results. Love and fear.
Love and fear.

Michael Leunig (b. 1945)
Australian writer and cartoonist

Never offer your heart to someone who eats hearts

Never offer your heart
to someone who eats hearts
who finds heartmeat
delicious
but not rare
who sucks the juices
drop by drop
and bloody-chinned
grins
like a God.

Never offer your heart
to a heart gravy lover.
Your stewed, overseasoned
heart consumed
he will sop up your grief
with bread
and send it shuttling
from side to side
in his mouth
like bubblegum.

If you find yourself
in love
with a person
who eats hearts
these things
you must do:

Freeze your heart
immediately.
Let him—next time
he examines your chest—
find your heart cold
flinty and unappetizing.

Refrain from kissing
lest he in revenge
dampen the spark
in your soul.

Now,
sail away to Africa
where holy women
await you
on the shore—
long having practiced the art
of replacing hearts
with God
and Song.

Alice Walker (b. 1944)
American writer

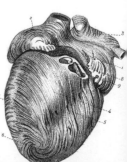

Chicken-Licken

She was afraid of men,
sin and the humors
of the night.
When she saw a bed
locks clicked
in her brain.

She screwed a frown
around and plugged
it in the keyhole.
Put a chain across
her door and closed
her mind.

Her bones were found
round thirty years later
when they razed
her building to
put up a parking lot.

Autopsy read:
dead of acute peoplelessness.

Maya Angelou (b. 1928)
American writer

Love

Loneliness, learning to do up her laces early,
    little knows
that love is, even now, about
to kill her.

Love plucks chickens.
Love plaits with skill its black rope of hair.
Like a Chinese grandmother. Look.

Love is a bound foot. How can it learn to
    walk
in a landscape without hope
like the Gobi Desert?

Love is arthritic and looks as if it would like
to strangle her. Love says:
' I would like to strangle you.

It is only a joke.'
Loneliness does up her shoes with a neat
    double knot.
Love is a wishbone, stuck, in her throat.

Gillian Allnutt (b. 1949)
English poet

Bloody Men

Bloody men are like bloody
    buses—
You wait for about a year
And as soon as one approaches
    your stop
Two or three others appear.

You look at them flashing their
    indicators,
Offering you a ride.
You're trying to read the
    destinations,
You haven't much time to decide.

If you make a mistake, there is no
    turning back.
Jump off, and you'll stand there
    and gaze
While the cars and the taxis and
lorries go by
And the minutes, the hours, the
days.

Wendy Cope (b. 1945)
English poet

Nerves

The modern malady of love is nerves.
Love, once a simple madness, now observes
The stages of his passionate disease,
And is twice sorrowful because he sees,
Inch by inch entering, the fatal knife.
O health of simple minds, give me your life,
And let me, for one midnight, cease to hear
The clock for ever ticking in my ear,
The clock that tells the minutes in my brain.
It is not love, nor love's despair, this pain
That shoots a witless, keener pang across
The simple agony of love and loss.
Nerves, Nerves! O folly of a child who dreams
Of heaven, and, waking in the darkness,
                    screams.

Arthur Symons (1865–1945)
English poet

Anxiety is love's greatest killer, because it is like the strange hold of the drowning.

Anaïs Nin (1903–77) American writer

Taiko Dojo
Messages from Haruko

No! No!
No. No. No. No.
No! No!
No. No. No. No.
No-No-No-No/No-No-No-No/No-
No-No-No

No-No-No-No
No! No!
No. No. No. No.
No! No!
No. No. No. No.
No-No-No-No/No-No-No-No
No-No-No-No
No! No!
No-No-No-No
No! No!

NO!

June Jordan (20th century)
American poet

15

16

WE DESIRE

THE WAY A TWICE-POISONED DOG

EYES A

THIRD PIECE OF MEAT

Philip Milito (20th century)
American poet

No one's land

Maybe this is the final battle
in the war between the man
and the woman, this great
and petty careful fight
between all the men and
all the women that we know:
someone, somewhere
is drawing up statements
for swearing and signing,
final surrender, honourable
peace. We have to go on
fighting, till the last break
or baby, fuck or hope, and after
that, in unarmed combat
of the oldest kind. I can

find no words or actions
that have not been used
before. I give myself up,
and only hesitate this side
of treachery, and only just.

Beyond this no one's land
I seek another, where
in being waywardly faithful
to just ourselves, we are
perfectly faithful
to each other. Till then
we mustn't promise anything.

Janet Dubé (b. 1941)
British poet

The terror is,
all promises are kept.

Robert Penn Warren (1905–88) American poet

The single woman considers herself

*A therapist once said that those people who appear
most independent are in fact the neediest, since
they see their needs and desires as too enormous to
be inflicted on others ...*

What a hippopotamus love
What a cavern of teeth
What a gobble
What a goat
What a snow-crusted lorry from the far north
What a mire in the handbag
What suitcases of dreams
What packing and unpacking
What a fat orange moon at the end of the night
What a lilac bush bursting in the green air
like God, like a rocket

Alison Fell (20th century)
Scottish poet

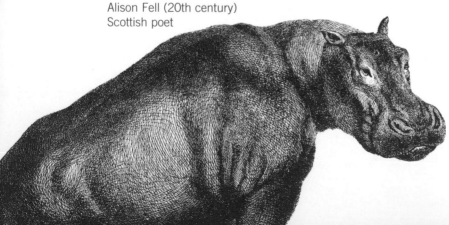

THERE WAS A DISTURBANCE

IN MY HEART, A VOICE

THAT SPOKE THERE AND SAID,

I WANT,

I WANT,

I WANT!

Saul Bellow (b. 1915)
American writer

19

Some Nights are Difficult for Me, Listen

Some nights are difficult for me, listen:
I want to talk about that hunger
that rises up in the old house;
I want to talk about the loneliness
that wakes at two a.m.
and stares at the deserted bed;
I want to talk about the sadness
of old clothes in the flea market,
and the tongues lost in tiny children;
I want to talk about the woman
who said she would meet me
at the theater and the part of me
that still waits for her; I want
to talk about how bullies
hurt the sweet heart, how
the heart walks in sleep, how
the heart hides in the clock,
hides in the hands of strangers;
I want to talk about this:
the wedding dress that poetry wore
one morning in the apple trees
so long ago, when she came to me,
innocent, distressed, and lovely.

James Tipton (20th century)
American poet

20

THIS, TO PONDER:

A HEART THAT'S SOLITARY

IS A HEART NO LONGER.

Antonio Machado (1878–1939)
Spanish poet

Words to her Lover

I shall keep this bit for God, she said,
tucking it away.

It could be a flower
or a star, a wooden spoon, rice
paper, the shine of the river
a common or garden stone—

You cannot see inside a stone, she
said.
It could be a moth
or a stamp with an African bird on it
a word I have forgotten
or a thin cloth folded like a
handkerchief
a leaf just looking
or the trick of an eyelid dreaming
a drop of cream, an apple
and a book on a rainy day
a wooden doll with one leg broken
since my birthday
or a thread in the eye of a needle.

Desist, she said,
mocking his open fist.
I have given you my bones to keep.

I will sleep like the earth in you.
I've given you my eyes, though
they are stones,
my apple heart with its green
sleeves.
I'll sing you a song like a river
flowing,
give you the sea that grieves in me
like broken things forgotten.
I would stir the earth for you
like a great wind blowing.

But I am going where the moon
goes now
when she has finished sewing up
the sky
and eats and eats stars
on the other side.

Give me the wooden spoon
so I can eat my curds and whey,
she said,
tucking in.

Gillian Allnutt (b. 1949)
English poet

21

Towards Silence
(extract)

I turn you out of doors
tenant desire

you pay no rent
I turn you out of doors
all my best rooms are yours
the brain and heart

                 depart
I turn you out of doors

switch off the lights
throw water on the fire
I turn you out of doors

stubborn desire

Alain Chartier (c.1385 until after 1433)
French writer and diplomat
Translated by Edward Lucie-Smith
(b. 1933) British Poet

Office Love

Office love, love of money and fight, love of calculated sex.
    The offices reek with thin volcanic metal. Tears fall in
    typewriters like drops of solder. Brimstone of bras-
    sieres, low voices, the whirr of dead-serious play. From
    the tropical tree and the Rothko in the Board Room to
    the ungrammatical broom closet fragrant with waxes,
    to the vast typing pool where coffee is being served by
    dainty waitresses maneuvering their hand trucks,
    music almost unnoticeable falls. The very telephones
    are hard and kissable, the electric water cooler sweetly
    sweats. Gold simmers to a boil in braceleted and sun-
    burned cheeks. What ritual politeness nevertheless,
    what subtlety of clothing. And if glances meet, if
    shoulders graze, there's no harm done. Flowers, cele-
    brations, pregnancy leave, how the little diamonds
    sparkle under the psychologically soft-colored ceilings.
    It's an elegant windowless world of soft pressures and
    efficiency joys, of civilized mishaps—mere runs in the
    stocking, papercuts.

Where the big boys sit the language is rougher. Phone calls
    to China and a private shower. No paper visible any-
    where. Policy is decided by word of mouth like gang-
    sters. There the power lies and is sexless.

Karl Shapiro (b. 1913)
American poet

The Answer

Why do you give the impression that you'd rather
not be loved? You almost tell people not to bother.
Why are you neither one thing nor the other?

Why do you fluctuate between ticks and crosses,
alternate between flippancy and neurosis?
Won't you confirm or contradict my guesses?

What is it that you do, by simply sitting
with your elbows raised, that makes me sick of waiting?
Why is your absence tantamount to cheating?

I know you're real, which means you must pay taxes,
catch colds and snore. I know you know what sex is.
Still, there is something in you that never mixes,

something that smells like the air in silver boxes.

It makes me suddenly afraid of asking,
suddenly sure of all the things I'm risking.

Sophie Hannah (20th century)
English poet

*I don't think I'll
dare to offer you my
hand, girl, this dirty,
twitching, clawlike,
unsteady, uncertain,
hot-cold hand.*

Franz Kafka
(1883–1924), Czech
writer, to Milena
Jesenská, early
1920s.

24

Happy love

Happy love. Is that normal,
is that serious, is that useful—
what does the world get out of two people
who don't see the world?

Lifted towards each other for no valid
      reason,
no different from a million others, but
      convinced
that it had to be thus—as reward for what?
      Nothing;
light falling from nowhere—
why on them and not on others?
Does this offend justice? Yes.
Does it upset solicitously piled principles,
does it upset morals? It does upset and
      topple them.

Look at these happy ones:
would they at least put on some disguise,
pretend a despondency to sustain their
      friends!
Hear how they laugh—offensively.
The language they use—seemingly
intelligible.

As for those ceremonies, the fuss,
their fanciful reciprocal duties—
they look like a conspiracy behind
      humanity's back!
It's hard to predict the outcome
if their example could be followed.
What would sustain religions and poets,
what would be remembered, what
      abandoned,
who would wish to stay within its
      bounds.
Happy love. Is it necessary?
It's tactful and sensible to ignore this
scandal in Life's higher spheres.
Fine babies are born without its
      assistance.
Never, never could it populate the earth,
given its rare occurrence.

Let people who haven't known happy
      love
insist it's nowhere to be found.

With such faith it'll be easier for them
      to live and to die.

Wislawa Szymborska (b. 1923), Polish poet, Translated by Adam Czerniawski

Statement

There are times, rares and few,
When contrary to all evidence,
Recorded pain, hearsay or exegesis
I believe that love is a window.

This is one of them
And I wish there were a few more around.

Feyyaz Fergar (1919–93)
Turkish poet, writer and translator

26

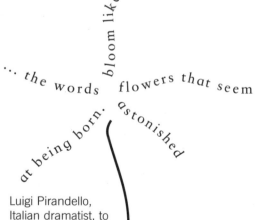

... the words *bloom like flowers that seem astonished at being born.*

Luigi Pirandello,
Italian dramatist, to
Marta Abba, an
actress, February
16th, 1931.

Love Comes Quietly

Love comes quietly,
finally, drops
about me, on me,
in the old ways.

What did I know
thinking myself
able to go
alone all the way.

Robert Creeley (b. 1926)
American poet

EXTRAVAGANT ARREARS OF MOONLIGHT YOU OWE ME

The Irresistible Desire to be Irresistibly Desired

The Business

To be in love is like going out-
side to see what kind of day

it is. Do not
mistake me. If you love

her how prove she
loves also, except that it

occurs, a remote chance on
which you stake

28

yourself? But barter for
the Indian was a means of
sustenance.

There are records.

Robert Creeley (b. 1926)
American poet

Calling

Every tune I turn
is for a love
an elusive Love
who touches me
and vanishes

I go about
singing so loud
that now and then
someone comes
for a while

James Berry (b. 1924)
Jamaican poet

Love consists in this, that two solitudes protect and touch and greet each other.

Rainer Maria Rilke (1875–1926) German poet

Symptoms of Love

Love is a universal migraine,
A bright stain on the vision
Blotting out reason.

Symptoms of true love
Are leanness, jealousy,
Laggard dawns;

Are omens and nightmares—
Listening for a knock,
Waiting for a sign.

For a touch of her fingers
In a darkened room,
For a searching look.

Take courage, lover!
Could you endure such grief
At any hand but hers?

Robert Graves (1895–1985)
English scholar, historian, essayist,
novelist and poet

Where does this tenderness come from?

Where does this tenderness come from?
These are not the—first curls I
have stroked slowly—and lips I
have known are—darker than yours

as stars rise often and go out again
(where does this tenderness come from?)
so many eyes have risen and died out
              in front of these eyes of mine.

and yet no such song have
I heard in the darkness of night before,
(where does this tenderness come from?):
              here, on the ribs of the singer.

Where does this tenderness come from?
And what shall I do with it, young
sly singer, just passing by?
Your lashes are—longer than anyone's.

Marina Tsvetayeva (1892-1941)
Russian poet
Translated by
Elaine Feinstein

29

E. Is In Love

What fire glows under her skirt! What
sparrow is gnawing at his heart!
The April air is slapping him
all the way home, the stupid trees
running after the awkward poem
circling his heart.
The stars are dust on the table
his dry throat is asking . . .

Go on, stupid heart, go on loving her.
Everything you do speaks like a mouth,
though you have nothing to say.
You wake up to words—table,
lipstick, balcony hanging like a tongue,
flower pot—objects, humble
like your heart: it's the world
that shouts her name!

The moon—tedium under his pillow.
The night—sprouting like a fountain.
His car—a matchbook holding its breath.
People—dry sticks poking through water.
The streets—question marks pointing nowhere.
His body, his living body, his blood
like ink & the pulley going crazy . . .

Ernesto Trejo (b. 1950)
American poet

*Love is an
irresistible
desire to be
irresistibly
desired.*

Robert Frost
(1874–1963)
American poet

30

Torture

—for Stephen Dobyns

You are falling in love again. This time
it is a South American general's daughter.
You want to be stretched on the rack again.
You want to hear awful things said to you
and to admit these things are true.
You want to have unspeakable acts
committed against your person, things
nice people don't talk about in classrooms.
You want to tell everything you know
on Simon Bolivar, on Jorge Luis Borges,
on yourself most of all.
You want to implicate everyone in this!
Even when it's four o'clock in the morning
and the lights are burning still—
those lights that have been burning night and day
in your eyes and brain for two weeks—
and you are dying for a smoke and a lemonade,
but she won't turn off the lights that woman
with the green eyes and little ways about her,
even then you want to be her gaucho.
Dance with me, you imagine hearing her say
as you reach for the empty beaker of water.
Dance with me, she says again and no mistake.
She picks this minute to ask you, hombre,
to get up and dance with her in the nude.
No, you don't have the strength of a fallen leaf,
not the strength of a little reed basket
battered by waves on Lake Titicaca.
But you bound out of bed
just the same, amigo, you dance
across wide open spaces.

Raymond Carver 1938–88) American writer

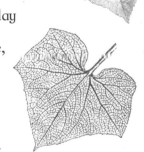

Thought

Love came to me and said:
What do you want of me?
Save me I said, Save me.
Love knelt down beside me
and love said:
If you knew the price
of coming to you,
you would ask nothing
but would give.

Henry Dumas (20th century)
American poet

Since that evening I have felt as though I had an opening in my ches

Franz Kafka (1883–1924), Czech write

The Love Poems
of Marichiko
(excerpt)

You ask me what I thought about
Before we were lovers.
The answer is easy.
Before I met you
I didn't have anything to think about.

Kenneth Rexroth (1905–82)
American poet

through which there was an unrestrained drawing-in and drawing-out.
Felice Bauer, November 1st, 1912.

The Old Words

This is hard to say
Simply, because the words
Have grown so old together:
Lips and *eyes* and *tears*,
Touch and *fingers*
And *love*, out of love's language,
Are hard and smooth as stones
Laid bare in a streambed.
Not failing or fading
Like the halting speech of the body
Which will turn too suddenly
To ominous silence,
But like your lips and mine
Slow to separate, our fingers
Reluctant to come apart,
Our eyes and their slow tears
Reviving like these words
Springing to life again
And again, taken to heart.
To touch, love, to begin.

David Wagoner (b. 1926)
American poet

LOVE

BEGETS

LOVE.

THIS

TORMENT

IS

MY

JOY.

Theodore Roethke
(1908–63)
American poet

Fortunato Pietro

Learning a new language is like
falling in love again That's why
the young are better at it: they
enter the field of the past
participle with no fear
of the tongue's betrayal

O my new love I am sorry
I stammer and falter
that I cannot always rise
al occasione But as I graze
among your suffixes
and prefixes your liquid

35

vocabolario and feminine
endings though my knees buckle
and my verbs freeze
my heart declines
to learn on its own: *O bella
molto bella bellisima!*

Peter Meinke (20th century)
American poet

Woman in Love

She is standing on my eyes
And her hair is in my hair;
She has the figure of my hands
And the colour of my sight.
She is swallowed in my shade
Like a stone against the sky.

She will never close her eyes
And will never let me sleep;
And her dreams in day's full light
Make the suns evaporate,
Make me laugh and cry and laugh,
Speak when I have nought to say.

Paul Eluard (1895–1952)
French poet
Translated by Gilbert Bowen

Love letter

Each touch would add a layer to my skin;
shared breath intensified the ether.
An alien heartbeat knocking at my chest, again,
that was blood stored up against the future.
What changed the body's mind, decreeing
that each withdrawal should be like the cork's—
a brief explosion, hiss of bubbles, leaving the bottle
less than it was?
           I don't know when the boys
began to walk away with parts of myself
in their sticky hands; when loving
became a process of subtraction. Or why,
having given up what seems so much,
I'm willing to lose even more—erasing
all this body's known, relearning it with you.

Melissa Stein (b. 1969)
American poet

Invaded by Souls

*"... but I'm always being invaded by others' souls
so I can't see my own soul very well."*
—*Shuntaro Tanikawa*

One night you fall asleep with an ungiven kiss
on your lips, you fall asleep in your kiss.
It is like sending yourself on an all night errand
to interview echoes about where they think
they're coming from. Where did it come from
anyway, your falling-asleep kiss? your
good-for-eternity soul?
How do you know they aren't imposters,
your unclouded kiss, your sublimated-soul?

To kiss and return a kiss is to be invaded
by souls, like a dead artist or a living poet,
like the twin sails of a ship in its sky-filled
sex act with the wind. Sometimes
we are taken charge of by the freedom of all those stones
children threw at nothing into the sky or into
the ocean from the Stone Age onward. We are
invaded by souls. We can't hold ourselves back
from each other then.

And besides, you've fallen asleep in your kiss.
Suddenly you are in a railway station
in a state of undress, naked except for your kiss
which, like your soul, is invisible and ungiven.
A whistle blows like a missed rendezvous with
the rest of your life. Souls are rushing past and into
you out of the vast Everything.

LOVE IS AN

ATTEMPT AT

PENETRATING

ANOTHER

BEING,

BUT IT

CAN ONLY

SUCCEED

IF THE

SURRENDER

IS MUTUAL.

Octavio Paz
(b. 1914)
Mexican poet

Moonlight You Owe Me

There is a dark frame around this absence
called "the dream." You are trying to exit
the wrong way down a stairwell invaded by souls.

You'd like to kiss your way out of this like a gangster
of the Starry Moment, but there are too many of them,
these lonely, imperishable souls rushing at you
full of desire and paradox, with wide pockets
of illumination and, as if to prove this is an American
dream and these are American souls,
some are riddled with bullets, cosmetically
punctuated with a certain brutal frankness.

But our capacity for love belongs to the birdsong
of antiquity which cleanses our dream-eyes and
allows them to mix moonlight with starlight
in those phosphorescent kisses multitudes
of plankton give the night.
They kiss with their whole beings, invisibly
sucking the fingertips of the dream's halflife.
Your own soul is in there too
filling up its tank on Infinite Joy and Diversity.
I don't know what else to tell you, except
you'll know when it happens.
A certain restless undulation as with waves
under fog. It's the souls, moving in.

Tess Gallagher (b. 1943)
American poet

Two bodies

Two bodies face to face
are at times two waves
and night is an ocean.

Two bodies face to face
are at times two stones
and night a desert.

Two bodies face to face
are at times two roots
laced into night.

Two bodies face to face
are at times two knives
and night strikes sparks.

Two bodies face to face
are two stars falling
in an empty sky.

Octavio Paz (b. 1914)
Mexican poet

Man the Barricades, the Enemy has let loose his Pyjamas!

yesterday
secure behind
your barricade
of polite coffeecups
you sat
whittling clichés

but lastnight
slyold me
got you up
some dark alleyway
of my dreams

this morning
you have a   faraway look
in your
smalltalk

Roger McGough (b. 1937)
English poet

Let Pleasure

Let pleasure burst through your
       heart
Let it knock you back
And thrill you with its aftershock
Let it spike down your centre
And your sex
And be happy
As a kebab on a hot skewer

Joan Woods (20th century)
English poet

Breath Poem No. 1

Excuse me miss,
      did you drop your breath
         into the road?
Breaths are very precious
      especially from those
         such as you.

—And so I ventured into the
world as her personal breath keeper.

Paul Nelson (20th century)
English poet

41

Communication

What I have to say to you is so
      private,
I can hardly bear,
For the words to be uttered,
Into the vacuous air,
So we take off our clothes.

Sasha Norris (20th century)
English poet

Requital

You wanted
to get inside me,
in my room
and in my heart
and in my life.

And I wanted
to get inside you,
too.

Terry Egan (20th century)
English poet

Jackie Kay (b. 1961) Scottish poet

Biography

She fell in love. Her heart opened and flapped
like so many pages in the wind. Everyday she got higher.
Smiling at the people bent over papers.
Grinning at the swots and the surreptitious
who scooped knowledge up in heavy armfuls,
and never shared it, nor said what they were doing.
Smiled at those who anxious, pulled out one book
then put it back and pulled out another.

My father caught me at it one day.
Radclyffe Hall dropped out from inside Bunty.
Page 106 was enough for him; he frog-marched me
down to the library where Cow Lick stammered,
'I thought it was for you,'
and my father disturbed the silence:
'What is the matter with you?' inbetween tight teeth.
My skin clung to my white blouse, innocence.
It was so hot, so hot. I nearly passed out.

She was in love. There was no turning back.
She took her letters to the library and read them
in between her book, so that she could read her lover
like a book, and get a thrill. A shiver
sung like wind through barley up and down her back.

'Darling,' they began in the middle
of A Glossary of Wood, 'I want you.'
Something in the silence named it.
She wrote back, her pen scratching and screaming,
'I'm wild about you, the slap and fetch of you.
You are my world, you know that don't you.'

December, 1903

And if I can't speak about my love—
if I don't talk about your hair, your lips, your eyes,
still your face that I keep within my heart,
the sound of your voice that I keep within my mind,
the days of September rising in my dreams,
give shape and colour to my words, my sentences,
whatever theme I touch, whatever thought I utter.

C. P. Cavafy (1863–1933)
Greek poet
Translated by Edmund Keeley and Philip Sherrard

43

Some Suggestions
Concerning You

The nearness of you is broken summer grasses;
The touch of you the seeding of the air
And our sneezes making cornflowers pollinate.

A whole kitchen is in your smell.
It secretes its ingredients in small places;
Busies itself in the clutter of my tongue and hands.

Your belly is a steamed august pear
Warming the soothed out cup of my palm,
Giving up the creased hub of its stem to a fingertip.

Your nipples are blueberries ripening in my mouth.
My cheek coasts the raw plantain of your sides;
I play my teeth in the freshly turned hay of your ribcage.

The neat walnut halves of your buttocks
And the small open fruit of the small of your back, are
Cultivating suggestions in the coarse grass of my groin.

Sarah Corbett (20th century)
English poet

WHAT YOU THINK

IS THE HEART

MAY WELL BE

ANOTHER ORGAN.

Jeanette Winterson
(b. 1959)
English writer

As Sweet

It's all because we're so alike—
Twin souls, we two.
We smile at the expression, yes,
And know it's true.

I told the shrink. He gave our love
A different name.
But he can call it what he likes—
It's still the same.

I long to see you, hear your voice,
My narcissistic object-choice.

Wendy Cope (b. 1945)
English poet

46

Direct Communication
(poet to secretary)

why paint your mouth
that pillarbox red
if you don't want
my letters popped in—

only mail can be expressed
with any degree of certitude
as to its delivery
to another

but I tell you I love
you don't you
understand I'm crazy
about the way you lick

stamps

Michael Horovitz (b. 1935)
German-born poet living in England

Their Attitudes Differ
(extract)

II
I approach this love
like a biologist
pulling on my rubber
gloves & white labcoat

You flee from it
like an escaped political
prisoner, and no wonder

III
A truth should exist,
it should not be used
like this. If I love you

is that a fact or a weapon?

Margaret Atwood (b. 1939)
Canadian writer

Platoon Commander

My mouth will have the ardours of Gehenna
My mouth will offer you a hell of sweetness and seduction
My mouth's angels will throne it in your heart
My mouth's soldiers will take you by assault
The priests of my mouth will cense your beauty
Your soul will tremble like land in an earthquake
Your eyes will be freighted with all the love that has gathered in
     men's eyes since the beginning
My mouth will be an army against you an incongruous jarring army
Protean like a magician who keeps changing his shape
The choirs and orchestra of my mouth will tell you my love
It murmurs to you now from far away
Meanwhile I stare at my watch and wait for the moment when we
     begin the assault

Guillaume Apollinaire (1880–1918)
French poet
Translated by Anne Hyde Greet

Lover

I don't just want
your heart
I want your flesh,
your skin
and blood and bones,
your voice, your thoughts
your pulse
and most of all your
fingerprints,

everywhere.

Nothing is more criminal
than love,
it steals hours from
the day,
dreams from my head,
the sun
from the sky,

perhaps it shone today,

I don't recall,
I distilled all your words
and made my own climate.

Isobel Thrilling (20th century)
English poet

I Wanted You in the Kitchen of My Heart

I wanted you in the kitchen of my heart;
and there, after many cold lunches,
I found you; and there, like herbs
undressing in soup, I came to love you;
and there, like a delicate tea
of mangoes and marigolds your mouth
opened, and your words, flecked with gold
and the eroticism of your Latin blood,
flowed, like the blood I longed for, into me.

And how could I lose you among these cups
and spoons, among these golden candles,
these jars of honey lined along the window?
And what forget-me-nots in winter
tie me to you still? I could die in this bread
I have made without you. For you I would burn
this dry brain for incense; I would
serve you the wine inside the night; I would
drink the sea to give you salt.

James Tipton (20th century)
American poet

49

Temptation

Call yourself alive? Look, I promise you
that for the first time you'll feel your pores opening
like fish mouths, and you'll actually be able to hear
your blood surging through all those lanes,
and you'll feel light gliding across the cornea
like the train of a dress. For the first time
you'll be aware of gravity
like a thorn in your heel,
and your shoulder blades will ache for want of wings.
Call yourself alive? I promise you
you'll be deafened by dust falling on the furniture,
you'll feel your eyebrows turning to two gashes,
and every memory you have—will begin
at Genesis.

Nina Cassian (b. 1924)
Romanian poet
Translation by Andrea Deletant and Brenda Walker

50

I'm Really Very Fond

I'm really very fond of you,
he said.

I don't like fond.
It sounds like something
you would tell a dog.

Give me love,
or nothing.

Throw your fond in a pond,
I said.

But what I felt for him
was also warm, frisky,
moist mouthed,
eager,
and could swim away

if forced to do so.

Alice Walker (b. 1944)
American writer

Arrears of Moonlight

My heart lies wrapped in red under your
          pillow,
My body wanders banished among the stars;
On one terrestrial pretext or another
You still withhold the extravagant arrears
Of moonlight that you owe me,
Though the owl whoops from a far olive
          branch
His brief, monotonous, night-long reminder.

Robert Graves (1895–1985)
English scholar, historian, essayist, novelist and poet

Valentine

Not a red rose or a satin heart.

I give you an onion.
It is a moon wrapped in brown paper.
It promises light
like the careful undressing of love.

Here.
It will blind you with tears
like a lover.
It will make your reflection
a wobbling photo of grief.

I am trying to be truthful.

Not a cute card or a kissogram.

I give you an onion.
Its fierce kiss will stay on your lips,
possessive and faithful
as we are,
for as long as we are.

Take it.
Its platinum loops shrink to a wedding-ring,
if you like.
Lethal.
Its scent will cling to your fingers,
cling to your knife.

Carol Ann Duffy (b. 1955)
Scottish-born English poet

BOTH WAYS
IS THE ONLY WAY
I WANT IT

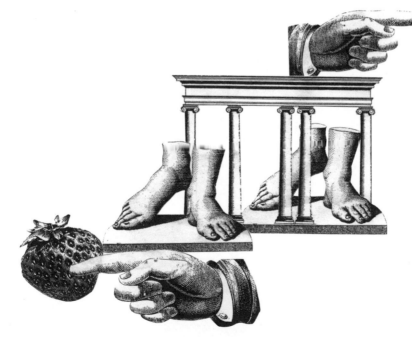

This Torment is my Joy

On the Roof

The trouble with me is that whether I get love or not
I suffer from it. My heart always seems to be prowling
a mile ahead of me, and, by the time I get there to surround it,
it's chewing fences in the next county, clawing
the bank-vault wall down or smashing in the window
I'd just started etching my name on with my diamond.

And that's how come I end up on the roof. Because even if I talk
into my fist everyone still hears my voice like the ocean
in theirs, and so they solace me and I have to keep
breaking toes with my gun-boots and coming up here
to live—by myself, like an aerial, with a hand on the ledge,
one eye glued to the tin door and one to the skylight.

C. K. Williams (b. 1936)
American poet

Better Not

Life
would perhaps
be easier
if I had
never met you

Less sadness
each time
when we must part
less fear
of the next parting
and the next after that

And not so much either
of this powerless longing
when you're not there

which wants only the
impossible
and that right away
next minute
and then
when that can't be
is hurt
and finds breathing difficult

Life
would perhaps be
simpler
If I hadn't met you
Only it wouldn't be
my life

Erich Fried (1921-88), Austrian poet

55

Coming Right Up

One can't
have it

both ways
and both

ways is
the only

way I
want it.

A. R. Ammons (b. 1926)
American poet

56

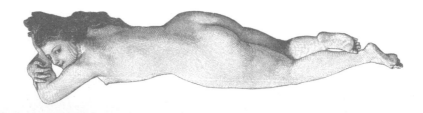

Love Affair

You walked into my landscape
and made revisions.

Dark cypresses were turned to catch
the sun's face,
meadows, going nowhere,
you stained with roadways
of return.

Pouring oil on my
matte turpentine,
you gave glow to opaque shadows.

Feeding flowers to a vase of
delft blue,
you changed my
still life.

Why are we perfect together?

I am adjustable.

Doris Klein (20th century)
American poet

57

"We Have a Crazy Love Affair"

We have a crazy love affair,
it is wanting each other to be happy.
Since nobody else cares for that
we try to see it ourselves.

Since everybody knows that sex
is part of love, we make love;
when that's over, we return
to shrewdly plotting the other's advantage.

Today you gazed at me, that spell
is like why I choose to live on.
God bless you who remind me simply
of the earth and sky and Adam.

I think of such things more than most
but you remind me simply. Man,
you make me proud to be a workman
of the Six Days, practical.

Paul Goodman (1911–72)
American poet

58

Reflection

I must balance
the unhappiness I suffer
because of you
against the happiness
you are to me

Does that go by days
and hours?
More weeks
of separation
of worry
of fear for you
and about you
than days of happiness?

But what use is counting?
I love you

Erich Fried (1921-88)
Austrian poet

59

This is to Let You Know

This is to let you know
That there was no moon last night
And that the tide was high
And that on the broken horizon glimmered the lights of ships
Twenty at least, like a sedate procession passing by.

This is to let you know
That when I'd turned out the lamp
And in the dark I lay
That suddenly piercing loneliness, like a knife,
Twisted my heart, for you were such a long long way away.

This is to let you know
That there are no English words
That ever could explain
How, quite without warning, lovingly you were here
Holding me close, smoothing away the idiotic pain.

This is to let you know
That all that I feel for you
Can never wholly go.
I love you and miss you, even two hours away,
With all my heart. This is to let you know.

Noël Coward (1899–1973)
English actor and playwright

The Taxi

When I go away from you
The world beats dead
Like a slackened drum.
I call out for you against the jutted stars
And shout into the ridges of the wind.
Streets coming fast,
One after the other,

Wedge you away from me,
And the lamps of the city prick my eyes
So that I can no longer see your face.
Why should I leave you,
To wound myself upon the sharp edges of the night?

Amy Lowell (1874–1925)
American Poet

61

I Want to Speak with the Blood that Lies Down

Yo quiero hablar con muchas cosas
y no me iré de este planeta
sin saber qué vine a buscar ... *
—*Pablo Neruda*

I want to speak with the blood that lies down
each night to sleep inside your heart; I want to speak
with these words that procreate like rabbits
when I think of you; I want to speak with your virginal ribs,
with the hand inside; I want to devour the mud that mocks
all diamond flesh; I want to find a prayer that sticks,
a clock that ticks only love, a time
that turns this desperation into peace, a book
with the moon on every page that only we

can read together; I want to speak in one
interminable sentence that can be understood
in a single sitting; I want to speak with
the tired angels that live inside the shoulders
of tiny children; I want to speak with cripples
that meet in laundromats late at night looking
for little boxes of soap; I want to speak with
these clothes before I join them; I want to find
the delicate violet that rises out of the dead volcano;
I want to find the v want to find the verb that shakes me loose,
the noun that is the place I live, the
comma that joins me with you; I want
to speak softly and thoroughly, and be clearly
in you; I want to speak with apples and honey
and silver and snow—*I want everything to stop*
for a moment destined for you and for me,
for a time when we butchered at birth

come back to life, rescued at last
like children in a miraculous fairy tale—
I want to speak with the dead, who move
like leaves in the night that blows its rapture
toward the dislocated sea; I want to speak
with the forgotten spring, with the light
in the dead comet; I want to speak with salt
and with the teeth I found in the desert and with
wounded silence, ravenous solitude;
I want to speak with Pablo Neruda and Christ,
and with the idiot brother of God, and with the tunnel
at the foot of the bed, with the corridors
of all longing; I want to speak with these long nights
of useless letters, with these boots that walk without me
when I rest, and with the spirits that shake these feet
when I lay me down to weep; I want to speak with the
thirsty rain, the lonely garbage, the tire that remembers
when it was a tree in Brazil; I want to speak with
the fragrance of sage that rises up, late into the night,
after a soft rain; I want to speak with cinnamon
and chocolate, and with windows that do not open,
and with the bag of hair in the shop of the old barber;
I want to speak with the dance that rises
in this body when, like a distant bell
come home, your letter rings in me whatever
matters; I want to whisper "love...love...love"
while this very hand is stretched to Sausalito,
cradling your heart in sleep.

> **I want to speak with many things*
> *and I will not leave this planet*
> *without knowing what I came to find...*

James Tipton (20=h century) American poet

A kiss on the head

A kiss on the head—wipes away misery.
I kiss your head.

A kiss on the eyes—takes away sleeplessness.
I kiss your eyes.

A kiss on the lips—quenches the deepest
thirst.
I kiss your lips.

A kiss on the head—wipes away memory.
I kiss your head.

Marina Tsvetayeva (1892-1941)
Russian poet
Translated by Elaine Feinstein

Forgetting Someone

Forgetting someone is like
forgetting to turn off the light in
the back yard
so it stays lit all the next day.

But then it's the light
that makes you remember.

Yehuda Amichai (b. 1924)
Israeli poet
Translated by Chana Bloch

BAD LOVE LAST LIKE A BIG UGLY LIZARD

When it is not Love Anymore

Poem About Heartbreak That Go On And On

bad love last like a big
ugly lizard crawl around the
house
forever
never die
and never change itself

into a butterfly

June Jordan (20th century)
American poet

The Mess of Love

We've made a great mess of love
Since we made an ideal of it.

The moment I swear to love a woman, a certain woman,
      all my life
That moment I begin to hate her.

The moment I even say to a woman: I love you!—
My love dies down considerably.

The moment love is an understood thing between us,
      we are sure of it,
It's a cold egg, it isn't love any more.

Love is like a flower, it must flower and fade;
If it doesn't fade, it is not a flower,
It's either an artificial rag blossom, or an immortelle,
      for the cemetery.

The moment the mind interferes with love,
      or the will fixes on it,
Or the personality assumes it as an attribute,
      or the ego takes possession of it,
It is not love any more, it's just a mess.
And we've made a great mess of love,
      mind-perverted, will-perverted,
      ego-perverted love.

D.H. Lawrence (1885–1930)
English writer

67

I am No Good at Love

I am no good at love
My heart should be wise and free
I kill the unfortunate golden goose
Whoever it may be
With over-articulate tenderness
And too much intensity.

I am no good at love
I batter it out of shape
Suspicion tears at my sleepless mind
And, gibbering like an ape,
I lie alone in the endless dark
Knowing there's no escape

I am no good at love
When my easy heart I yield
Wild words come tumbling from my mouth
Which should have stayed concealed;
And my jealousy turns a bed of bliss
Into a battlefield.

I am no good at love
I betray it with little sins
For I feel the misery of the end
In the moment that it begins
And the bitterness of the last good-bye
Is the bitterness that wins.

Noël Coward (1899–1973)
English actor and playwright

68

Trenchwarfare

after the battle of the Incriminating Loveletter
there came an uneasy truce
We still sleep together in the same trench
but you have built
a wall of sandbags in between

somenights
gutsy and fullofight
rifle in hand
I'm over the top
brave asa ram

and you're always waiting,
my naked sentry
'Halt, who goes there? Friend or lover?'
'Lover'
'Advance lover'

in the morning
whistling 'itsalongwaytotipperary'
i trudge across the skyline
to the bathroom

Roger McGough (b. 1937)
English poet

I rather look

upon love

altogether as

a sort of

hostile

transaction.

69

George Gordon,
Lord Byron,
English poet,
to an unknown
woman,
November 10th,
1822.

T e a s e

I will give you all my keys,
    You shall be my châtelaine;
You shall enter as you please,
    As you please shall go again.

When I hear you jingling through
    All the chambers of my soul,
       How I sit and laugh at you
In your vain housekeeping rôle.

Jealous of the smallest cover,
    Angry at the simplest door;
Well, you anxious, inquisitive lover,
Are you pleased with what's in store?

You have fingered all my treasures,
    Have you not, most curiously,
Handled all my tools and measures
    And masculine machinery?

Over every single beauty
    You have had your little rapture:
    You have slain, as was your duty,
Every sin-mouse you could capture.

    Still you are not satisfied,
Still you tremble faint reproach;
    Challenge me I keep aside
Secrets that you may not broach.

    Maybe yes and maybe no,
    Maybe there are secret places,
    Altars barbarous below,
Elsewhere halls of high disgraces.

    Maybe yes and maybe no.
    You may have it as you please,
    Since I choose to keep you so,
Suppliant on your curious knees.

D.H. Lawrence (1885–1930), English writer

Stubborn Kisses

This kiss won't ride in a car
even with you
in the back seat looking dangerous
as mink. It insists
on running alongside the window
like a piece of the scenery
that won't give you up.

See that splatter, right
where you thought for a moment
it was beautiful? Insects
die over and over
just to prove the sky
is lived-in like this heart
for which I have been given
an inferior sign.

Soon you'll get tired, worrying
about the car running over
my feet, worrying
for the child in me
that's attracting
all these mothers
like a bad parade. You'll
tell the driver to stop
and let you out.

I'll let you
out. I'll stop
and let you out.

Tess Gallagher (b. 1943)
American poet

A blade of grass

You ask for a poem.
I offer you a blade of grass.
You say it is not good enough.
You ask for a poem.

I say this blade of grass will do.
It has dressed itself in frost,
It is more immediate
Than any image of my making.

You say it is not a poem,
It is a blade of grass and grass
Is not quite good enough.
I offer you a blade of grass.
You are indignant.

You say it is too easy to offer grass.
It is absurd.
Anyone can offer a blade of grass.

You ask for a poem.
And so I write you a tragedy about
How a blade of grass
Becomes more and more difficult
          to offer,

And about how as you grow older
A blade of grass
Becomes more difficult to accept.

Brian Patten (b. 1946)
English poet

LOVE NEVER DIES OF STARVATION, BUT OFTEN OF INDIGESTION.
Ninon de Lenclos (1620–1705)
French courtesan

When I Mentioned Love

She said, *fetch me a plaster*,
So I ran headlong
To the bathroom cabinet
And sped back
Fearing she had done herself injury.
She took it
And stuck it
Right across my mouth.

Simon Marshall (20th century)
English poet

You looked for a flower ...
(untitled)

73

You looked for a flower
and found a fruit.
You looked for a well
and found a sea.
You looked for a woman
and found a soul—
you are disappointed.

Edith Södergran (1892–1923)
Finnish poet
Translated by David McDuff

Wearing the Collar

I live with a lady and four cats
and some days we all get
along.

some days I have trouble with
one of the
cats.

other days I have trouble with
two of the
cats.

other days,
three.

some days I have trouble with
all four of the
cats

and the
lady:

ten eyes looking at me
as if I was a dog.

Charles Bukowski (b. 1920 –1994)
American writer

a Big Ugly Lizard

Repentence must come. It is the after-taste of passion.
Mary Braddon (1837–1915) English novelist

Acts of Contrition

There's you, behind the red curtain,
waiting to absolve me in the dark.
Here's me, third in the queue outside
the same deep green velvet curtain.
I'm working on my confessional tone.

Here's me opening my wrists
before breakfast, Christmas day,
and here's you asking if it hurt.
Here's where I choose between *mea culpa*
and *Why the hell should I tell you?*

Me again, in the incident room this time,
spitting my bloody teeth into your palm.
I could be anyone you want me to be.
I might come round to your point of view.

Michael Donaghy (b. 1954)
American poet

Song for A Beautiful Girl Petrol-Pump Attendant on the Motorway

I wanted your soft verges
But you gave me the
                hard shoulder.

Adrian Henri (b. 1932)
English poet

Like a Baby

Your love is killing mine.
You love me
too passionately.

Why should I make any effort?
You weep enough for us both
with your desire and your jealousy.

Your love grows more and more beautiful,
you're the mystical bush in Dante's paradise,
a fountain of ecstatic flames
that towers above me
more bravely every day.

You flourish
in your suffering. While I'm withering away
like a limb
that isn't used.

I've already forgotten what it means to suffer.
I'll soon have the spiritual life
of a baby.

Anna "Swir" (1909–84)
Polish poet
Translated by Margaret Marshment and Grazyna Baran

DON'T YOU
KNOW THAT TO
LOVE
EXCESSIVELY
BRINGS BAD
LUCK TO LOVER
AND BELOVED?
IT'S LIKE
OVERFONDLED
CHILDREN:
THEY DIE
YOUNG.

Gustave Flaubert,
French writer, author
of Madame Bovary,
to Louise Colet,
French poet,
August 9th, 1846.

My Bed

I like to leave it rumpled,
pillows strewn, sheets tossed
from one side to the other,
the duvet dripping on the floor,
looking steamy,
even though you haven't touched me
for a week.

Ann Gray (20th century)
English poet

♥ 77

Their Sex Life

One failure on
Top of another

A. R. Ammons (b. 1926)
American poet

Revelation

Your love is darkening my star—
the moon is rising in my life.
My hand is not at home in yours.
Your hand is lust—
my hand is longing.

Edith Södergran (1892–1923)
Finnish poet
Translated by David McDuff

78

Misunderstanding

They had the look of lovers
Who'd spent the night together.

Reluctantly they parted
To go their working ways.

She walked and turned to wave.
He went on unaware.

He walked and turned to wave.
She went on unaware.

Now each of them thinks
The other one loves less.

Tom Earley (b. 1911)
Welsh poet

I Dream

Erich Fried (1921-88) Austrian poet

I dream I am living
I dream I have got to know you
(quite suddenly, quite unexpectedly, as if that were possible)
I dream that we love each other

I dream that we still love each other
I dream you meet another man
I dream you love him but tell him
you still want to love me too
I dream he says he understands
and we can go on loving each other
(as if that were possible)

I dream he says he finds it difficult
(not quite suddenly and not quite unexpectedly)
I dream you say you will try
to turn our love into mere friendship
but that you want still to have that friendship
I dream he says he understands
(as if that were possible)

I dream I have come to terms with this
I dream life goes on and work
I dream you speak to him about everything
and he to you about everything the way you wanted
I dream he puts up with our friendship
and that if we are not all dead
today we still go on living happily ever after
(as if that were possible)

The Lady Next Door

The lady next door,
Who weighs eight pounds less than I do
And wears peach face gleamer and tawny lip
        gloss to take out the garbage,
Has lately been looking at my husband
As if he were someone like Robert Redford,
And she were someone like Ali MacGraw,
And I were someone like Mother of the Year.

The lady next door,
Whose children go to analysts and Choate,
And whose favorite drink is a dry white burgundy
        with a smidgin of crème de cassis,
Has lately been looking at my husband
As if he were someone with inexpressible
        yearnings,
And she were someone who majored in how to
        express them,
And I were someone who played a lot of
        hockey.

The lady next door,
Has lately been looking at my husband,
Who has lately been looking back,
Leaving me to contemplate
Murder,
Suicide,
Adult education courses,
An affair with one of those rich Greek eighty-
        year-olds who prefer younger women,
An affair with one of those alienated twenty-year-
        olds who prefer older women,

Or maybe an affair
With the man next door,
Who has Cardin suits, a rapier wit, a Ferrari,
As well as close friends in the arts,
And who has lately been looking at me
As if I were someone who knew how to sew on
      buttons,
And he were someone who needed someone to
      sew them,
And my husband were only someone who
      deserved
The lady next door.

Judith Viorst (b. 1931)
American writer

Song of Affluence or I Wouldn't Leave my 8-roomed House for You

I wouldn't leave my little 8-roomed house for you
I've got one missus and I don't want two

I love you baby but you must understand
That feeling's fine and kissing you's grand
But I wouldn't leave my little wooden wife for you

Water tastes fine but money tastes sweeter
I'd rather have a fire than a paraffin heater
And
I wouldn't change my little 8-roomed life for you.

Adrian Henri (b. 1932)
English poet

The Turkish Carpet

No man could have been more unfaithful
To his wife than me;
Scarcely a day passed
That I was not unfaithful to her.
I would be in the living room ostensibly reading or writing
When she'd come home from work unexpectedly early
And, popping her head round the door, find me wrapped round
A figure of despair.
It would not have been too bad if I'd been wrapped round
Another woman—that would have been infidelity of a kind
With which my wife could have coped.
What she could not cope with, try as she did,
Was the infidelity of unhope,
The personal betrayal of universal despair.
When my wife called to me from the living-room door
Tremblingly ajar, with her head peering round it—
The paintwork studded with headwounds and knuckleprints—
Called to me across the red, red grass of home—
The Turkish Carpet—
Which her gay mother had given us as a wedding present
(And on which our children had so often played
Dolls' houses on their hands and knees
And headstands and cartwheels and dances,
And on which we ourselves had so often made love),
I clutched my despair to my breast
And with brutality kissed it—Sweet Despair—
Staring red-eyed down at *The Turkish Carpet.*
Oh my dear husband, will you not be faithful to me?
Have I not given you hope all the days of my life?

82

Paul Durcan (b 1944) Irish poet

Buttons

Perhaps you don't love me at all,
but at least you sew buttons on my coat
which is more than my wife does.

Adrian Henri (b. 1932)
English poet

Telling the same story twice
(untitled)

83

Telling the same story twice
doesn't make it any the less true

so long as one remembers whom
one has already told it to

except when one is telling lies
in which case the reverse applies

I love you, I love you, I love you.

Kate Thomas (20th century)
English poet

Land of Fog

In winter my love
is among the beasts of the forest.
The vixen knows
I must be back before morning
and she laughs.
How the clouds tremble! And a layer
of brittle ice falls
on my snow collar.

In winter my love
is a tree among trees
and invites the hapless crows
to nest in her beautiful boughs. She knows
that the wind, when evening falls,
will lift her stiff, frost-embroidered
evening dress and chase me home.

In winter my love
is among the fish and cannot speak.
A slave to the waters her fins
stroke from within,
I stand on the bank and watch,
till ice floes drive me away,
how she dives and turns.

And struck once more by the hunting cry
of the bird stiffening
his wings above me, I fall
on an open field: she plucks
the hens and tosses me a white
collar bone. I place it around my neck
and go forth through the bitter down.

Faithless is my love,
I know, sometimes she sways
on high heels into town,
kissing bar glasses with her straw
deep in their mouths,
finding the right words for everyone.
But I don't understand this language.

It is fog land I have seen,
fog heart I have eaten.

Ingeborg Bachman (1926–1973)
German poet and novelist
Translated by Mark Anderson

My Heart is Lame

My heart is lame with running after yours so fast
        Such a long way,
Shall we walk slowly home, looking at all the things we passed
        Perhaps to-day?

Home down the quiet evening roads under the quiet skies,
        Not saying much,
You for a moment giving me your eyes
        When you could bear my touch.

But not to-morrow. This has taken all my breath;
        Then, though you look the same,
There may be something lovelier in Love's face in death
As your heart sees it, running back the way we came;
        My heart is lame.

Charlotte Mew (1869–1928)
English Writer

85

heart note

because we for a while had been living there my heart

thought it was a house with cupboards and an open fire
and a door giving onto
an impossible steep twisted stair my heart

thought it could have small uncurtained windows it could go on
being there under its tiles for the swallows
every year

love was already living in the house my heart

thought when we got there it thought it was
a letterbox a back door opening to
a garden it could walk in

it was nothing we had put there but before us it was

apple willow and a wilderness of
rose thorn thick and dark
and light with its daylong delicate flowers my heart

thought it had roots it thought it could cover its roots
with straw it thought it could carry on
lighting its every morning fire

because we as love for a while had been living there

Gillian Allnutt (b. 1949)
English poet

In Return

I know you think
you love me. One night,
when your loneliness was storming,
the idea of love was born.
Everything became quiet, the night
had that washed, clean smell.
The rain stopped.

I remember your tenderness
toward me. You scrubbed floors,
cleaned house, made love to me
with your love
in mind. I became lazy.

But this wasn't enough.
You wanted me quiet
while it talked, wanted
to let it tear through the house
like a spoiled child
determining our lives. Even now

you shout at me
if I question you
about your love, its habit
of locking doors, making more
noise than a storm—

making you lonely in return.

Sheila Zamora (1947-1978)
American poet

it may not always be so;
and i say

it may not always be so;and i say
that if your lips,which i have loved,should touch
another's,and your dear strong fingers clutch
his heart,as mine in time not far away;
if on another's face your sweet hair lay
in such a silence as i know,or such
great writing words as,uttering overmuch,
stand helplessly before the spirit at bay;

if this should be,i say if this should be—
you of my heart,send me a little word;
that i may go unto him,and take his hands,
saying,Accept all happiness from me.
Then shall i turn my face,and hear one bird
sing terribly afar in the lost lands.

e.e. cummings (1894–1962)
American poet

Farewell

sadness

Good morning

sadness.

Paul Éluard
(1895–1952)
French poet

GODDAMN
THE EMPTY SKY

You've Left Me

Home is where the heart is

I made a home for you in my heart.
it didn't have four walls
but it had a door
so you left

Jade Reidy (20th century)
English poet

90

Prescience

Had I known that the heart
breaks slowly, dismantling itself
into unrecognizable plots of
misery,

Had I known the heart would leak,
slobbering its sap, with a vulgar
visibility, into the dressed-up
dining rooms of strangers,

Had I known that solitude could
stifle the breath, loosen the joint,
and force the tongue against the
palate,

Had I known that loneliness could
keloid, winding itself around the
body in an ominous and beautiful
cicatrix,

Had I known, yet I would have loved
you, your brash and insolent beauty,
your heavy comedic face
and knowledge of sweet
delights,

But from a distance.
I would have left you whole and wholly
for the delectation of those who
wanted more and cared less.

Maya Angelou (b. 1928)
American poet

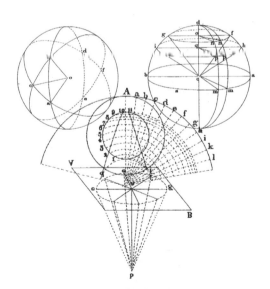

To Burn Out Love

To burn out love is to burn a star
        from the sky
But can touch reach so far,
Feel the fire increase
Careful the heart but not the star
        will burn?

Star that pulsates like a fish:
My heart meets you in dark or light
To taste the waters of the star which says:
Trust once gone can never be restored—
Such love can surely be put out,
The power to break its fire with my fist.

Allan Sillitoe (b. 1928)
English writer

The Save the Redwoods League

At the tree museum
At the arboretum,
Is a cross-section of
        an old giant redwood
(or, *Sequoia Sempervirens*),
Whose chronological rings
Recycle continuous time
From discontinuous time:
'An Historical Consciousness
From The Petrified Forest' . Look—
Here's the Battle of Hastings, the
Signing of the Magna Carta, and
The Battle of Saratoga from
The American Civil War.
And see—
Here's that day you told me
You didn't love me anymore.

A.C. Bevan (20th century)
English poet

CLEAN!

'CLEAN!'
you spelled out: 'Make it'/'Break it
clean!'
But you meant <u>mean</u>
as in

<u>mean</u>
<u>hard</u>
<u>gone</u>

like how you done me

<u>mean</u>
<u>hard</u>
<u>gone</u>
<u>hard</u>

<u>done</u>

June Jordan (20th century)
American poet

A Pity. We Were Such
a Good Invention

They amputated
your thighs from my hips.
As far as I'm concerned, they're always
doctors. All of them.

They dismantled us
from each other. As far as I'm concerned,
they're engineers.
A pity. We were such a good and loving
invention: an airplane made of a man and a woman,
wings and all:
we even got off
the ground a little.
We even flew.

Yehuda Amichai (b. 1924)
Israeli poet
Translated by Stephen Mitchell

What Hurts

If I lose you
what
is it
that hurts me?

Not my head
nor my body
nor my arms
nor my legs

They are tired
but they don't hurt
or no worse
than the one leg always does

Breathing doesn't hurt
It is a little tight
but less
than with a cold

My back doesn't hurt
nor does my stomach
my kidneys don't hurt
nor does my heart

Why then
can't I bear
to lose you?

Erich Fried (1921-88)
Austrian poet

Felicity in Turin

We met in the Valentino in Turin
And travelled down through Italy
            by train,
Sleeping together.
I do not mean having sex.
I mean sleeping together.
Of which sexuality is,
And is not, a part.
It is this sleeping together
That is sacred to me.
This yawning together.
You can have sex with anyone
But with whom can you sleep?

I hate you
Because having slept with me
You left me.

Paul Durcan (b. 1944)
Irish poet

95

Overheard By A Young Waitress

Three thirty-fivish women met one day,
each well glossed against the others' sharp eyes for flaws.
Old school friends apparently—they slipped
with ease into the former conspiracy of dormitories,
and discussed over coffee and saccharine, the grounds
for divorce. All agreed love made
excessive demands on them,
wondered how long it must be missing
before it could be
                    Presumed Dead.

Liz Lochhead (b. 1947)
Scottish poet

Half

You make the toast, love,
easily on this last day,
feathering it gently
with butter. Accommodating
to the last I chop fresh
red sticks of purest cinnammon
and sprinkle it like confetti
evenly on the toasted slice,
half for you
and half for me.

We eat it smoothly like oil.
Half for you, half for me
and later the furniture too
and even perhaps the children.
Love ends in half.

Karen Hayes
(20th-century)
American-born English poet

97

Love Is Finished Again

Love is finished again, like a profitable citrus season
or like an archaeological dig that turned up
from deep inside the earth
turbulent things that wanted to be forgotten.

Love is finished again. When a tall building
is torn down and the debris cleared away, you stand there
on the square empty lot, saying: What a small
space that building stood on
with all its many floors and people.

From the distant valleys you can hear
the sound of a solitary tractor at work
and from the distant past, the sound of a fork
clattering against a porcelain plate,
beating an egg yolk with sugar for a child,
clattering and clattering.

Yehuda Amichai (b. 1924)
Israeli poet
Translated by Chana Bloch

Upon the Intimation of Love's Mortality

It is the effort of the lie
Exacts a wounding pulse.
I loved you much
When everything had excellence at once.
First was our freshness and the stun of that.
Your body raved with music. What was lost
Is just that element our time always takes
And always in love we venture off some height
That nothing else can equal after it.
The thought of that bedevils me for miles.
How can I save you from my own despair
To think I may not love you as before?
Spoiled, we become accustomed to our luck.
This is the devil of the heart.
We were the smiles of gods awhile
And now, it seems, our ghosts must eat us up
Or wail in temples till our tombs are bought.
Attended now by shades of that great while,
Disguise is the nature of my guile
And yet the lie benumbs the soul.
Get me the purity of first sight!
Or strength to bear the truth of after light!

Jean Garrigue (1912–72)
American poet

After That

Do you know how much pain is left
in the world? One tiny bit of pain is left,
braised on one cell like a toothmark.
And how many sorrows there still are? Three sorrows:
the last, the next to the last and this one.

And there is one promise left, feeling
its way through the poison, and one house
and one gun and one shout of agony
that wanders in the lost cities and the lost mountains.
And so this morning, suffering the third sorrow

from the last, feeling pain in my last gene,
cracks in the struts, bubbles in the nitro,
this morning for someone I'm not even sure exists
I waste tears. I count down by fractions
through the ash. I howl. I use up everything.

C. K. Williams (b. 1936)
American poet

100

E m p t y   S k y

Violeta Parra (1917–67) Chilean writer

Goddamn the Empty Sky

Goddamn the empty sky
and the stars at night
goddamn the ripply bright
stream as it goes by
goddamn the way stones lie
on dirt or on the street
goddamn the oven's heat
because my heart is raw
goddamn the laws
of time the way they cheat
my pain's as bad as that.

Goddamn the mountain chain
the Andes and the Coast
goddamn Mister the most
and least amount of rain
also crazy and sane
and candour and deceit
goddamn what smells so sweet
because my luck is out
goddamn the lack of doubt
what's messy and what's neat
my pain's as bad as that.

Goddamn the Spring
with its plants in blossom
and the color of Autumn
goddamn the whole damn thing
birds on the wing
goddamn them more and more
'cause I'm really done for
goddamn Winter to bits
along with Summer's tricks
goddamn the saint and whore
my pain's as bad as that.

Goddamn getting on your feet
for the stars and stripes
goddamn symbols of all types
Venus and Main Street
and the canary's tweet
the plants and their motions
the earth with its erosions
because my soul is sore
goddamn the ports and shores
of the enormous oceans
my pain's as bad as that.

Goddamn the moon and weather
desert and river bed
goddamnit for the dead
and the living together
and the bird with all its feathers
is such a goddamn mess
schools, places to confess
I tell you what I'm sick of
goddamn that one word love
with all its nastiness
my pain's as bad as that.

So goddamn the number eight
eleven nine and four
choir boys and monsignors
preachers and men of state
goddamn them it's too late
free man and prisoner
soft voice and quarreler
I damn them every week
in Spanish and in Greek
thanks to a two-timer
my pain's as bad as that.

Nothing

To your abandonment I have opposed
my godlike tower of intelligence.
I climb up there; my blood-stained heart has caused
the sea to be empurpled with its sense.

I'll manufacture dawn from my old shadow,
protect my lyre from vain and wanton winds,
search in my self for my own sustenance; . . .
but, ah, if that sweet peace should bring me nothing!

102

Nothing, yes, nothing, nothing! Oh that the waters
might now receive my soul; and in this manner
the world be one great prison, chill and naught!

For you are you; you are the human spring,
of earth, air, water, fire—of everything;
while I myself am nothing but my thought.

Juan Ramón Jiménez (1881–1958)
Spanish poet

Little Words

When you are strayed, there is nor bloom nor leaf
  Nor singing sea at night, nor silver birds.
And I may only stare, and shape my grief
  In little words.

I cannot conjure loveliness, to drown
  The bitter woe that racks my chords apart.
The staggering pen that sets my sorrow down
  Feeds at my heart.

There is no mercy in the shifting year;
  No beauty wraps me tenderly about.
I turn to little words—so you, my dear,
  Can spell them out.

Dorothy Parker (1893–1967)
American writer

103

How the Bloom
Leaves the Rose

You
don't send
me

flowers
            anymore
                    fuckface.

Andre Segui (20th century)
English poet

A Dog After Love

After you left me
I had a bloodhound sniff at
my chest and my belly. Let it fill its nostrils
and set out to find you.

I hope it will find you and rip
your lover's balls to shreds and bite off his cock—
or at least
bring me one of your stockings between its teeth.

Yehuda Amichai (b. 1924)
Israeli poet
Translated by Chana Bloch

My heart is turned to stone; I strike it,

William Shakespeare (1564–1616)

You Thought I Was That Type

You thought I was that type:
that you could forget me,
and that I'd plead and weep and throw myself
under the hooves of a bay mare,

or that I'd ask the sorcerers
for some magic potion made from roots
and send you a terrible gift:
my precious perfumed handkerchief.

Damn you! I will not grant
your cursed soul vicarious tears
      or a single glance.
And I swear to you by the
      garden of the angels,
I swear by the miracle-working ikon,
and by the fire and smoke of our nights:
I will never come back to you.

Anna Akhmatova (1889-1966)
Russian poet
Translated from Russian by Richard McKane

Dance of Murder

I'm leaving.

You didn't make me suffer
so you needn't expect
my hatred.
That would be too splendid
      and important a gift.
You're not worth anything
as precious
as a shred of living flesh.

I've killed
your presence within me,
easily.

I'm cleansed.
I'm dancing a festive dance of murder.

Anna "Swir" (1909–84)
Polish poet
Translated by Margaret Marshment
and Graznya Baran

105

and it hurts my hand.

Havisham

Beloved sweetheart bastard. Not a day since then
I haven't wished him dead. Prayed for it
so hard I've dark green pebbles for eyes,
ropes on the back of my hands I could strangle with.

Spinster. I stink and remember. Whole days
in bed cawing Nooooo at the wall; the dress
yellowing, trembling if I open the wardrobe;
the slewed mirror, full-length, her, myself, who did this

to me? Puce curses that are sounds not words.
Some nights better, the lost body over me,
my fluent tongue in its mouth in its ear
then down till I suddenly bite awake. Love's

hate behind a white veil; a red balloon bursting
in my face. Bang. I stabbed at a wedding-cake.
Give me a male corpse for a long slow honeymoon.
Don't think it's only the heart that b-b-b-breaks.

Carol Ann Duffy (b. 1955)
Scottish-born English poet

The Heart (excerpt)

In the desert
I saw a creature, naked, bestial,
Who, squatting upon the ground,
Held his heart in his hand
And ate of it.
I said, "Is it good, friend?"
"It is bitter—bitter," he answered;
"But I like it
Because it is bitter,
And because it is my heart."

Stephen Crane (1871–1900)
American writer

h e a r t   i s   m o s t l y   h e a r t .

american writer

Thinking of You

I spent last night burning all your letters.
Today I stray from room to room and try
To remember your last address, and whether
I promised your faithful hamster would die

Smashed against the walls, which incidentally
Are magnolia now, magnolia all the way
Because you loathed it. And environmentally
Sound, undyed toilet rolls have had their day.

My trolley shrieks with rolls of every hue:
Apricot, strawberry, peach. I like to think
That when, in your memory, I flush the loo,
Gradually a warm, suggestive, pink
Will spread across the long, cold miles of sea,
And you will look at it, and think of me.

Sam Gardiner (20th century)
English poet

Good of Love

Four years she ate my dinners
Four years she drank my wines
And all the while
I was nourishing her
For some other crummy swines.

Spike Milligan (b. 1918)
English comedian and poet

The All-Purpose Country and Western Self-Pity Song

He jumped off the box-car
in Eastbourne, the beast born
in him was too hungry to hide:

His neck in grief's grommet
He groaned through his vomit
As the churn
And the yearn
At the turn
Of the tide.

He headed him soon
For a sad-lit saloon
In back of the edge of the strand,
Where a man almost ended
Sat down and extended

His speckled,
Blue-knuckled
And cuckolded
Hand.

Cried, The wind broke my marriage in
two.
Clean through the bones of it,
Christ how it blew!
I got no tomorrow
And sorrow
is tough to rescind:
So forgive me if I should break wind,
son,
Forgive me
If I should break wind.

At this the bartender
Addressed the agenda,
A dish-cloth kept dabbing his eye.
Said, Pardon intrusion

Upon your effusion
Of loss but none wooed it
Or rued it
As I.

For after the eve of Yvonne,
My God, how it hurts now the woman
has gone!

Heart-sick as a dog,
I roll on like a log
Down the roaring black river
Where once sailed
A swan.

Then the dog on the floor,
Who'd not spoken before,
Growled, Ain't it the truth you guys
said?
I may be a son-
Of-a-bitch but that bitch

Was my Sun
And she dumped me,
That bitch did,
For dead.

So three lonely guys in the night and a
hound
Drank up, and they headed them out to
the Sound
Threw up, then they threw themselves
In and they
Drowned.

O dee-o-dayee . . .
O dee-o-dayee . . .
Woe-woe-dalayee . . .

Kit Wright (b. 1944) English poet

Like the Inner Wall of a House

Like the inner wall of a house
that after wars and destruction becomes
an outer one—
that's how I found myself suddenly,
too soon in life. I've almost forgotten what it means
to be inside. It no longer hurts;
I no longer love. Far or near—
they're both very far from me,
equally far.

I'd never imagined what happens to colours.
The same as with human beings: a bright blue drowses
inside the memory of dark blue and night,
a paleness sighs
out of a crimson dream. A breeze
carries odors from far away
but itself has no odor. The leaves of the squill die
long before its white flower,
which never knows
the greenness of spring and dark love.

I lift up my eyes to the hills. Now I understand
what it means to lift up the eyes, what a heavy burden
it is. But these violent longings, this pain of
never-again-to-be-inside.

Yehuda Amichai (b. 1924)
Israeli poet
Translated by Chana Bloch

110

Mythistorema

I woke with this marble head in my hands;
it exhausts my elbows and I don't know where to put it down.
It was falling into the dream as I was coming out of the dream
so our life became one and it will be very difficult for it
                to separate again.

I look at the eyes: neither open nor closed
I speak to the mouth which keeps trying to speak
I hold the cheeks which have broken through the skin
I haven't got any more strength.

My hands disappear and come toward me
mutilated.

George Seferis (1900–72)
Greek poet
Translated by Edmund Keeley
and Philip Sherrard

112

The memory of you emerges from the night around me.
The river mingles its stubborn lament with the sea.

Deserted like the wharves at dawn.
It is the hour of departure, oh deserted one!

Cold flower heads are raining over my heart.
Oh pit of debris, fierce cave of the shipwrecked.

In you the wars and the flights accumulated.
From you the wings of the song birds rose.

You swallowed everything, like distance.
Like the sea, like time. In you everything sank!

It was the happy hour of assault and the kiss.
The hour of the spell that blazed like a lighthouse.

Pilot's dread, fury of a blind diver,
turbulent drunkenness of love, in you everything sank!

In the childhood of mist my soul, winged and wounded.
Lost discoverer, in you everything sank!

You girdled sorrow, you clung to desire,
sadness stunned you, in you everything sank!

I made the wall of shadow draw back,
beyond desire and act, I walked on.

Oh flesh, my own flesh, woman whom I loved and lost,
I summon you in the moist hour, I raise my song to you.
Like a jar you housed the infinite tenderness,
and the infinite oblivion shattered you like a jar.

There was the black solitude of the islands,
and there, woman of love, your arms took me in.

There were thirst and hunger, and you were the fruit.
There were grief and the ruins, and you were the miracle.

Ah woman, I do not know how you could contain me
in the earth of your soul, in the cross of your arms!

E m p t y   S k y

How terrible and brief was my desire of you!
How difficult and drunken, how tensed and avid.

Cemetery of kisses, there is still fire in your tombs,
still the fruited boughs burn, pecked at by birds.

Oh the bitten mouth, oh the kissed limbs,
oh the hungering teeth, oh the entwined bodies.

Oh the mad coupling of hope and effort
in which we merged and despaired.

And the tenderness, light as water and as flour.
And the word scarcely begun on the lips.

This was my destiny and in it was the voyage of my longing,
and in it my longing fell, in you everything sank!

Oh pit of debris, everything fell into you,
what sorrow did you not express, what waves did not
drown you.

From billow to billow you still called and sang.
Standing like a sailor in the prow of a vessel.

You still flowered in songs, you still broke in currents.
Oh pit of debris, open and bitter well.

Pale blind diver, luckless slinger,
lost discoverer, in you everything sank!

It is the hour of departure, the hard cold hour
which the night fastens to all the timetables.

The rustling belt of the sea girdles the shore.
Cold stars heave up, black birds migrate.

Deserted like the wharves at dawn.
Only the tremulous shadow twists in my hands.

Oh farther than everything. Oh farther than everything.

It is the hour of departure. Oh abandoned one!

Pablo Neruda (1904–73) Chilean poet

You Came Last Season

You came and made penny candies with your thumbs
I stole you and ate you
And my feet crushed your wrappers
       in a thousand streets
You hurt my teeth
You put pimples on my face
You were never anything for health
You were never too vitamin
You dirtied hands
And since you were stickier than glue
And never washed away
You stained something awful.

Gregory Corso (b. 1930)
American poet

114

Letter to a Kiss
That Died for Us

I have been writing your memoir.
It is like leaving this world
and still finding you there
as you received us, shaped us
and instantly became unrepeatable.
I keep thinking I can write a cheek against
you, if not lips. A magnetic cheek
with the taste of cold, metallic air
on it so the clang of it will stay
a little after. I tempt you with nakedness
on a terrace, with tambourines, all my gypsy
favors. With the sleek flanks of longing,
I tempt you who are gone forever,
a thought I can have
as this letter is written
outside any death.

Tess Gallagher (b. 1943)
American poet

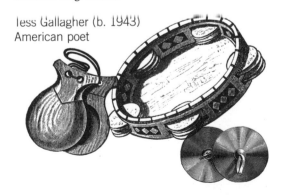

postscriptcard

This is where we were
when the moon
nipped at us.
I've marked the bed-
room with a cross.
Believe me,
we were cheap, we were
in heaven, we were
forgetting how to lie.
Wish I was here. Love
Me

Alison Fell (20th century)
Scottish poet

So Many Times I Have Felt the Sea Rising

So many times I have felt the sea rising
in my heart, when in my hands
I hold your letters, like singing nets of words
lifted out of some blue solitude for me alone.

So many times again I open your golden letters,
reading them to bees, to canyon walls,
to tiny lizards that dart like thoughts
through these deserts of perpetual loneliness.

So far away, so far, I felt, wanting to live at last
with only spirits, but *oh, dueña del amor*,
the feather I found, fallen from the angel's wing,
means nothing to me now.

James Tipton (20th century)
American poet

AFTER YEARS OF LISTENING,

A S T O N E
COMES TO LIFE

I Will No Longer Apologize for Loving You

Hash Wednesday

last wednesday
  it all clicked

  you only wanted me for my loveandaffection
                          my generosity
                  and my undyingfaithfulness

(to you my prizegiven rosaries meant nothing,
my holy relics, merely relics)

Begone oh Belial's daughter
I wash my hands of you in holy water

next year i will live alone
and breed racehorses
in the attic

Roger McGough (b. 1937)
English poet

How Have I Been

since you last saw me?
Well,
        I've never been lonely
        I've danced at parties,
        and drunk flat beer
with other men;
        I've been to the cinema and seen
        one or two films you would have liked
with other men;
        I've passed the time in amusement arcades
        and had one or two pretty fruitless
        goes on the fruit machine;
        I've memorised the patterns
        of miscellaneous neckties.
Indifferent, I
        put varying amounts of sugar
in different coffee cups
        and adjusted myself to divers heights
        of assorted goodnight kisses, but
my breasts (once bitten)
                shy away from contact
I keep a curb
                on mind and body—
Love? I'm no longer
                        exposing myself.

Liz Lochhead (b. 1947)
Scottish poet

And Please Do Not Presume

And please do not presume it was the way we planned it,
Nor later say *We might have tried harder,*
Or *Could have done better.*
Nor remind us of the things we didn't take:
The hints, the trains, the tonics,
The tape-recordings of ourselves asleep,
The letters of a previous lover,
The photos of each other as a child.

And please do not presume our various ways of making up,
Of telling lies and truths, the way we touched
Or laughed, the Great Mistakes, the Tiger Suit,
Our list of *Twenty Favourite Movie Classics,*
Breakfast in bed, red wine, the different ways we tried
To make each other come
Were anything else than the love we wanted;

Or that we did no more or less than anybody might have done.

And more, do not presume we could have stopped it—
Like a clock, a gap, a leak, or rot; or made it
Last much longer than it did;
Or that the note on the fridge that one of us left,
Wasn't sweetly mean, but badly spelt:
Step One of *Ten Proggressive Ways to Disolution.*

Deryn Rees-Jones (20th century)
English poet

120

The End of Love

The end of love should be a big event.
It should involve the hiring of a hall.
Why the hell not? It happens to us all.
Why should it pass without acknowledgement?

Suits should be dry-cleaned, invitations sent.
Whatever form it takes—a tiff, a brawl—
The end of love should be a big event.
It should involve the hiring of a hall.

Better than the unquestioning descent
Into the trap of silence, than the crawl
From visible to hidden, door to wall.

Get the announcement made, the money spent.
The end of love should be a big event.
It should involve the hiring of a hall.

Sophie Hannah (20th century)
English poet

Tonight I Can Write

Tonight I can write the saddest lines.

Write, for example, 'The night is starry
and the stars are blue and shiver in the distance'

The night wind revolves in the sky and sings.

Tonight I can write the saddest lines.
I loved her, and sometimes she loved me too.

Through nights like this one I held her in my arms.
I kissed her again and again under the endless sky.

She loved me, sometimes I loved her too.
How could one not have loved her great still eyes.

Tonight I can write the saddest lines.
To think that I do not have her. To feel that I have lost her.

To hear the immense night, still more immense without her.
And the verse falls to the soul like dew to the pasture.

What does it matter that my love could not keep her.
The night is starry and she is not with me.

This is all. In the distance someone is singing. In the distance.
My soul is not satisfied that it has lost her.

My sight tries to find her as though to bring her closer
My heart looks for her, and she is not with me.

The same night whitening the same trees.
We, of that time, are no longer the same.

I no longer love her, that's certain, but how I loved her.
My voice tried to find the wind to touch her hearing.

Another's. She will be another's. As she was before my kisses.
Her voice, her bright body. Her infinite eyes.

I no longer love her, that's certain, but maybe I love her.
Love is so short, forgetting is so long.

Because through nights like this one I held her in my arms
my soul is not satisfied that it has lost her.

Though this be the last pain that she makes me suffer
and these the last verses that I write for her.

Pablo Neruda (1904–73), Chilean poet

123

Tess Gallagher (b. 1943) American poet

124

Elegy with a Blue Pony

It is said one-third of China
is a cemetery: "But what
a cemetery!" Henri Michaux exclaimed.
Somewhere a cemetery exists
for all the kisses I was going to
give you. Multitudes of butterflies
like to sleep there in that third
of my heart's country. Their wings
open and shut pensively, as if
the lips of the sky had come down
to announce the end of a journey,
to ruffle the meadow grass
with the azure breeze of the moment.

If, in your travels in the spirit world,
you suddenly recall those kisses you
might have had, you won't have to
live again to enjoy them.
They are waiting. You will always
be expected by my kisses.
Lie down. Let the nose
of my blue pony brush your neck.
Don't be sad I'm not with her, or
that the butterflies rise as a body
to let her pass. Don't be sad.
I'm still alive and have to follow
my kisses around. But you, you can
lie down and be enlivened, kissed
into yet another imperishable
collaboration on the way to me.

I So Liked Spring

I so liked Spring last year
   Because you were here;—
    The thrushes too—
Because it was these you so liked to hear—
    I so liked you.

   This year's a different thing,—
    I'll not think of you.
But I'll like Spring because it is simply Spring
    As the thrushes do.

Charlotte Mew (1869–1928)
English Writer

125

After Years of Listening,
A Stone Comes to Life

After years of listening, a stone comes to life,
and the candle in the tiny grass;
and the night, like a wife, comes home;
a feather, in this touch of wind, flies back
to the lost bird, and everything I do not know
begins to sway at once.

I love these nights of irresistable somnambulance!
These nights when the wind blows its lullaby
to each lonely wing; I love this old body I walk in,
I love this dependable sage, this desert scent
I sink into when I rest; and suddenly I know
I will no longer apologize for loving you.

I whispered your name and the wind whinnied back.
All the horses of heaven are in the pasture tonight.

James Tipton (20th century)
American poet

Acknowledgements

Every effort has been made to locate all copyright-holders. In the event that he have unwittingly or unwillingly omitted the proper notification, we would be grateful to hear from the copyright-holder, and undertake to amend any further editions accordingly.
The editors gratefully acknowledge permission to reprint the following poems:

"You Thought I Was That Type" from Anna Akhmatova: Selected Poems, translated by Richard McKane, published by Bloodaxe Books. Translation © 1989 Richard McKane. Reprinted by permission of Bloodaxe Books Ltd. "Love" and "Heart Note" from Blackthorn by Gillian Allnutt, published by Bloodaxe Books. © 1994 Gillian Allnutt. Reprinted by permission of Bloodaxe Books Ltd. "Words to her Lover" from Spitting the Pips Out by Gillian Allnutt, first published by Sheba Feminist Publishers. © 1981 Gillian Allnutt. Reprinted by permission of the author. "A Dog After Love", "A Pity. We Were Such a Good Invention", "Like the Inner Wall of a House", "Forgetting Someone" and "Love is Finished Again" from The Selected Poetry of Yehuda Amichai, edited and translated by Chana Bloch and Stephen Mitchell, published by the University of California Press. © The Regents of the University of California. English translations © 1986 Chana Bloch and Stephen Mitchell. "Their Sex Life" and "Coming Right Up" from The Really Short Poems of A.R. Ammons. © 1990 A.R. Ammons. Reprinted by permission of W.W. Norton & Company, Inc. "Chicken-Licken" from Oh Pray My Wings Are Gonna Fit Me Well, by Maya Angelou. © 1975 Maya Angelou. Reprinted by permission of Random House, Inc. and published in Great Britain in The Complete Collected Poems of Maya Anglou, published by Virago Press. © 1994 Maya Angelou. Reprinted by permission of Little, Brown. "Prescience" from Shaker, Why Don't You Sing by Maya Angelou. © 1983 Maya Angelou. Reprinted by permission of Random House, Inc. and published in Great Britain in The Complete Collected Poems of Maya Anglou, published by Virago Press. © 1994 Maya Angelou. Reprinted by permission of Little, Brown. "Platoon Commander" from Calligrammes by Guillaume Apollinaire, translated by Anne Hyde Greet, published by the University of California Press. © 1980 The Regents of the University of California. Extract from "Their Attitudes Differ" from Power Politics by Margaret Atwood. ©1971 House of Anansi Press Ltd. Reprinted by permission of Stoddart Publishing Co. Ltd, Canada. "Land of Fog" from In the Storm of Roses: Selected Poems by Ingeborg Bachmann, translated, edited and introduced by Mark Anderson, published by Princeton University Press. English translation © 1986 Mark Anderson. Reprinted by permission of the translator. Originally published in German by Piper Verlag. "Calling" from Fractured Circles by James Berry, published by New Beacon Books Ltd. © 1979 James Berry. "The Save the Redwoods League" by A. C. Bevan. © 1998 A. C. Bevan. Reprinted by permission of the author. "Wearing the collar" from You Get So Alone At Times That It Just Makes Sense by Charles Bukowski, published by Black Sparrow Press. © 1986 Charles Bukowski. Reprinted by permission of Black Sparrow Press. "Torture" from Fires: Essays, Poems, Stories by Raymond Carver. First published in Great Britain in 1985 by Collins Harvill and in the USA by Vintage, a Division of Random House, Inc. © 1968, 1969, 1970, 1971, 1972, 1973, 1974, 1975, 1976, 1977, 1978, 1979, 1980, 1981, 1982, 1983, 1984, 1991 Tess Gallagher. Reproduced by permission of The Harvill Press and Random House, Inc. "Temptation" from Call Yourself Alive? by Nina Cassian, translated by Andrea Deletant and Brenda Walker, published by Forest Books in 1988, reprinted in 1989 and 1992. © 1988 Nina Cassian. Translation © 1988 Brenda Walker and Andrea Deletant. "December, 1903" from Collected Poems by C.P. Cavafy, translated by Edmund Keeley and Philip Sherrard, edited by George Savidis, published by Chatto & Windus. © 1963 and 1968 Kyveli A. Singopoulo. Reprinted on behalf of the estate of C.P. Cavafy by permission of Rogers, Coleridge and White and Random House UK Ltd. Poem by Alain Chartier from Towards Silence, translated by Edward Lucie-Smith, published by Oxford University Press. © 1968 Edward Lucie-Smith. Reprinted by permission of Rogers, Coleridge and White on behalf of the author. "As Sweet" and "Bloody Men" from Serious Concerns by Wendy Cope. Reprinted by permission of Faber & Faber Publishers Inc. and Faber & Faber Ltd. © 1992 Wendy Cope. "Some Suggestions Concerning You" by Sarah Corbett, published in The West in Her Eye, Poems by Women, edited by Rachel Lever, published by

Pyramid Press. © Sarah Corbett. "You Came Last Season" from The Vestal Lady on Brattle by Gregory Corso, first published by Richard Brukenfeld, Cambridge, Massachusetts in 1955. Reprinted by permission of City Lights Bookstore. © 1955 Gregory Corso. "I am No Good at Love" and "This is to Let You Know" from Noël Coward: Collected Verse, published by Methuen London. © 1984 the Estate of the late Noël Coward. "Love Comes Quietly" and "The Business" published in the USA in The Collected Poems of Robert Creeley 1945–1975 by The University of California Press, © 1983 The Regents of the University of California, and published in the Great Britain in Poems 1950–1965 by Marion Boyars Publishers Ltd. © 1962 Robert Creeley. Reproduced by permission of Marion Boyars Publishers Ltd. "it may not always be so,and i say" from Complete Poems 1904–1962 by E.E. Cummings, edited by George J. Firmage, by permission of W.W. Norton & Company Ltd. © 1923, 1951, 1976, 1991 by the Trustees for the E.E. Cummings Trust and George James Firmage. "Acts of Contrition" from Errata by Michael Donaghy, reprinted by permission of Oxford University Press. © 1993 Michael Donaghy. "No one's Land" by Janet Dubé from Dancing the Tightrope, edited by Barbara Burford, Lindsay McRae and Sylvia Paskin, published by The Women's Press. © 1987 Janet Dubé. Reprinted by permission of the author. "Valentine" and "Havisham" from Mean Time by Carol Ann Duffy, published by Anvil Press Poetry Ltd. © 1993 Carol Ann Duffy. "Thought" from Knees of a Natural Man by Henry Dumas, published by Thunder's Mouth Press. © 1989 Loretta Dumas and Eugene B. Redmond. Used by permission of Thunder's Mouth Press. "The Turkish Carpet" and "Felicity in Turin" from A Snail In My Prime by Paul Durcan, first published in Great Britain by Harvill in 1993. © 1993 Paul Durcan. Reprinted by permission of The Harvill Press. "Misunderstanding" from All These Trees by Tom Earley, published by Gomer Press. © 1992 Tom Earley. "Requital" by Terry Egan. © 1998 Terry Egan. Reprinted by permission of the author. "Woman in Love" from Selected Poems by Paul Eluard, selected and translated by Gilbert Bowen, published by Calder Publications. © Calder Publications. Reprinted by permission of the Calder Educational Trust. "The single woman considers herself" and "postscriptcard" from The Crystal Owl by Alison Fell, published by Methuen, London. © 1988 Alison Fell. Reprinted by permission of Peake Associates. "Complaints and confessions of a poem" by Feyyaz Fergar from The Bright is Dark Enough, A cycle of poems of dark ecological introspection, published by The Rockingham Press. ©1993 the estate of Feyyaz Fergar.
"Statement" by Feyyaz Fergar from A Talent for Shrouds, published by The Rockingham Press. ©1991 the estate of Feyyaz Fergar. "What Hurts", "Reflection", "Anti-Litany" and "I Dream" from Love Poems by Erich Fried, published by Calder Publications, London and Riverrun Press Inc, New York . © 1979 and 1983 Verlag Klaus Wagenabach and this translation © 1991 Stuart Hood. Permission to reprint granted by the Erich Fried Estate and the Calder Educational Trust, London. "Stubborn Kisses", "Letter to a Kiss That Died for Us", "Elegy with a Blue Pony" and "Invaded by Souls" by Tess Gallagher. © 1992, 1994 Tess Gallagher. "Thinking of You" by Sam Gardiner, first published in The Poetry Review, Vol. 84, no 4. © 1994 Sam Gardiner. Reprinted by permission of the author. "Upon the Intimation of Love's Mortality" from Countries Without Maps by Jean Garrigue, published by Macmillan Publishing Corp. © 1964 Jean Garrigue. Reprinted by permission of the Estate of Jean Garrigue. "We Have a Crazy Love Affair" from Collected Poems by Paul Goodman, published by Random House in 1972. © 1972 Paul Goodman. Reprinted by permission of Sally Goodman. "Arrears of Moonlight" and "Symptoms of Love" from Poems About Love by Robert Graves, first published by Cassell plc. in 1969. © 1958, 1959, 1960, 1961, 1962, 1963, 1964, 1965, 1966, 1967, 1968 The Executors of the Estate of Robert Graves. Reprinted by permission of Carcanet Press Ltd. "My Bed" from Painting Skin by Ann Gray, published by Fatchance Press. © 1995 Ann Gray. "The Answer" from Second Helping of Your Heart by Sophie Hannah, published by Crabflower Pamphlets. © 1994 Sophie Hannah. "The End of Love" from The Hero and the Girl Next Door by Sophie Hannah, published by Carcanet Press Ltd. © 1995 Sophie Hannah. Reprinted by permission of the author. "Half" from Between Mornings by Karen Hayes, published by Stride Publications. © 1995 Karen Hayes. "Buttons" and "Song for a Beautiful Girl Petrol-Pump Attendant on the Motorway" from The Best of Henri, first

127